Doggie Data

CHRISTA C. HOGAN

WORLD BOOK

This World Book edition of *Yorkshire Terriers*
is published by agreement between
Black Rabbit Books and World Book, Inc.

2140 Howard Dr. West,
North Mankato, MN 56003 U.S.A.
World Book, Inc.,
180 North LaSalle St., Suite 900,
Chicago, IL 60601 U.S.A.

Marysa Storm, editor; Catherine Cates, interior designer; Grant Gould, cover designer; Omay Ayres, photo researcher

Library of Congress Control Number: 2017016406

ISBN: 978-0-7166-3450-8

Printed in China. 3/18

Image Credits

Alamy: CROSSEMY VANESSA, 16 (bloodhound); Libby Welch, 14 (bttm dog); Tierfotoagentur, 1, 15 (full pg); iStock: Lilithoas, 19; sshepard, 18; tiggi, 14 (top); Shutterstock: Africa Studio, 23 (top); Amber Earnest, 21 (adolescent); Anna Goroshnikova, 10 (full pg big dog, bkgd); Bernhard Richter, [illegible] (adult); Bill Anastasiou, 31; Bogdan Sicovski, 13 (bttm); Cian Suebsri, 14 (bttm bkgd), 20 (puppy bkgd); dien, 8–9; Eric Isselee, Cover (dog), 10–11 (bttm dogs); Jarry, 6; Javier Brosch, Cover (doghouse); Jim Vallee, 22; Karelnoppe, 3; Kukuruxa, 17 (terrier); Lee Swash, 32; Margarita Zhuravleva, 4–5; Phase4Studios, 27; Scorpp, 23; Stephen Mcsweeny, 24; Stueber, 20 (dog); Suberl, 6–7; Svetography, 17 (spaniel); tsik, 17 (terrier); Vivienstock, 17 (beagle); Will Rodrigues, 10 (terrier); Ygapko, 28

Every effort has been made to contact copyright holders for material reproduced in this book. Any omissions will be rectified in subsequent printings if notice is given to the publisher.

Contents

CHAPTER 1

Meet the

A Yorkshire terrier **prances** down the street next to its owner. Its **silky** hair is tied up in a bright red bow. People stop to admire the small dog. When a larger dog walks by, the Yorkie is not afraid. It barks out a greeting. This dog is all about confidence.

20 25 30
15
35
10
40
5
45
0
50
pounds
pounds
WEIGHT
7 POUNDS
(3 kilograms)
or less

Sweet and Little

Yorkies are a toy dog breed. In 2016, these tiny dogs were the most popular toy dog in America. It is not hard to see why. Yorkies have beauty and brains. These smart dogs make **loyal**, loving pets.

How Big Is a Yorkshire Terrier?

HEIGHT
at shoulder
6 TO 9
INCHES
(15 to 23 centimeters)

PARTS OF A YORKSHIRE TERRIER

BRIGHT EYES

BUTTON NOSE

SHORT, POINTED EARS

HAIRLIKE COAT

TOP 10
MOST POPULAR
Dogs in the United
States in 2016
1
Labrador
Retrievers
2
German
Shepherds
3
Golden
Retrievers
4
Bulldogs

CHAPTER 2

A Special

Despite their small size, Yorkies have a lot of energy and big attitudes. Yorkies aren't afraid of larger dogs. They like to chase squirrels too. Yorkies also like to be the boss. Owners must be careful. A spoiled Yorkie will take over the house!

Happy Homes

Yorkies need a lot of attention. They love to cuddle and play. But they don't need a lot of space for exercise. Their size makes them a good fit for families in apartments.

Homes with little kids may not be a good choice for Yorkies, though. Yorkies are easily hurt by rough play. Young kids may not understand how to handle small dogs.

Yorkies dislike the cold. They need to bundle up in winter!

Yorkies love to bark, especially at strangers. This makes them good watchdogs.

Yorkie Challenges

Yorkies are smart dogs. They're easy to train. But owners often let these small pups get away with things most big dogs can't. Because Yorkies make smaller messes and have quieter barks, owners may ignore bad behavior. If owners let puppies misbehave, these dogs can develop bad **habits**.

CHAPTER 3

Yorkshire Terriers'

Yorkies are known for their bright eyes. They have soft, straight hair. It is tan and black.

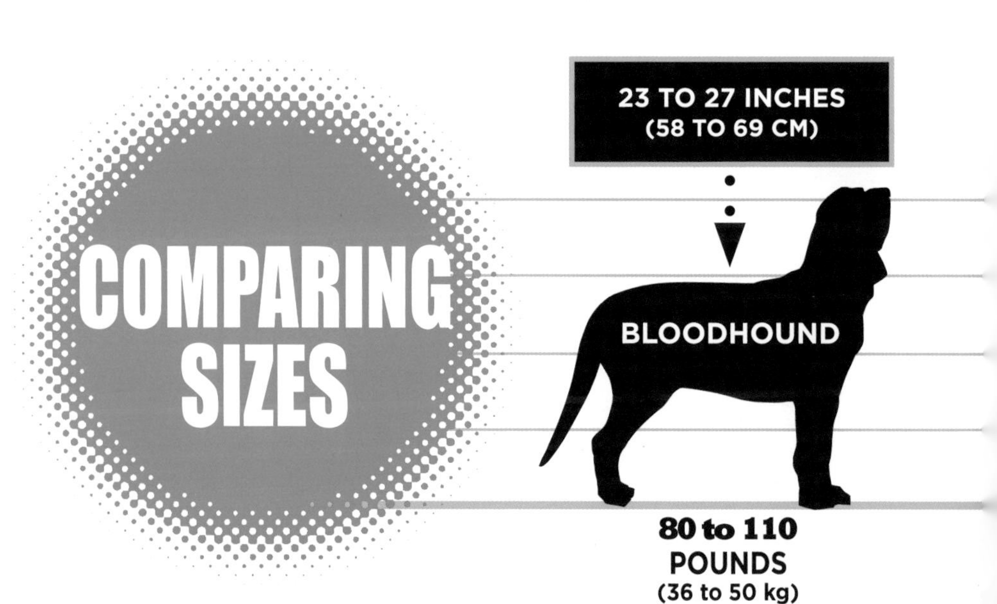

13.5 TO 15.5 INCHES
(34 TO 39 CM)
13 TO 15 INCHES
(33 to 38 CM)
6 TO 9 INCHES
(15 TO 23 CM)
COCKER
SPANIEL
BEAGLE
YORKSHIRE
TERRIER
20 to 30
POUNDS
(9 to 14 kg)
18 to 30
POUNDS
(8 to 14 kg)
POUNDS

Yorkies live
12 to 15 years.

Yorkshire Terrier Health

Yorkies are usually healthy dogs. But all dogs can have health problems, especially as they age. Yorkies can get eye diseases. Sometimes they **dislocate** their knees. Dislocated knees make it painful for them to walk.

Yorkshire Terrier Life Cycle

Newborn Yorkies are tan and black.

Senior Yorkies sleep more and move more slowly.

Yorkies' coats get lighter as they age.

Many Yorkies are playful even when they're fully grown.

CHAPTER 4

Caring for Yorkshire Terriers

Yorkies are small dogs, but they take a lot of work. Their soft, hairlike coats tangle easily. The coats can be trimmed short or left long. Either way, Yorkies need to be brushed every day. The dogs need baths weekly.

Grooming

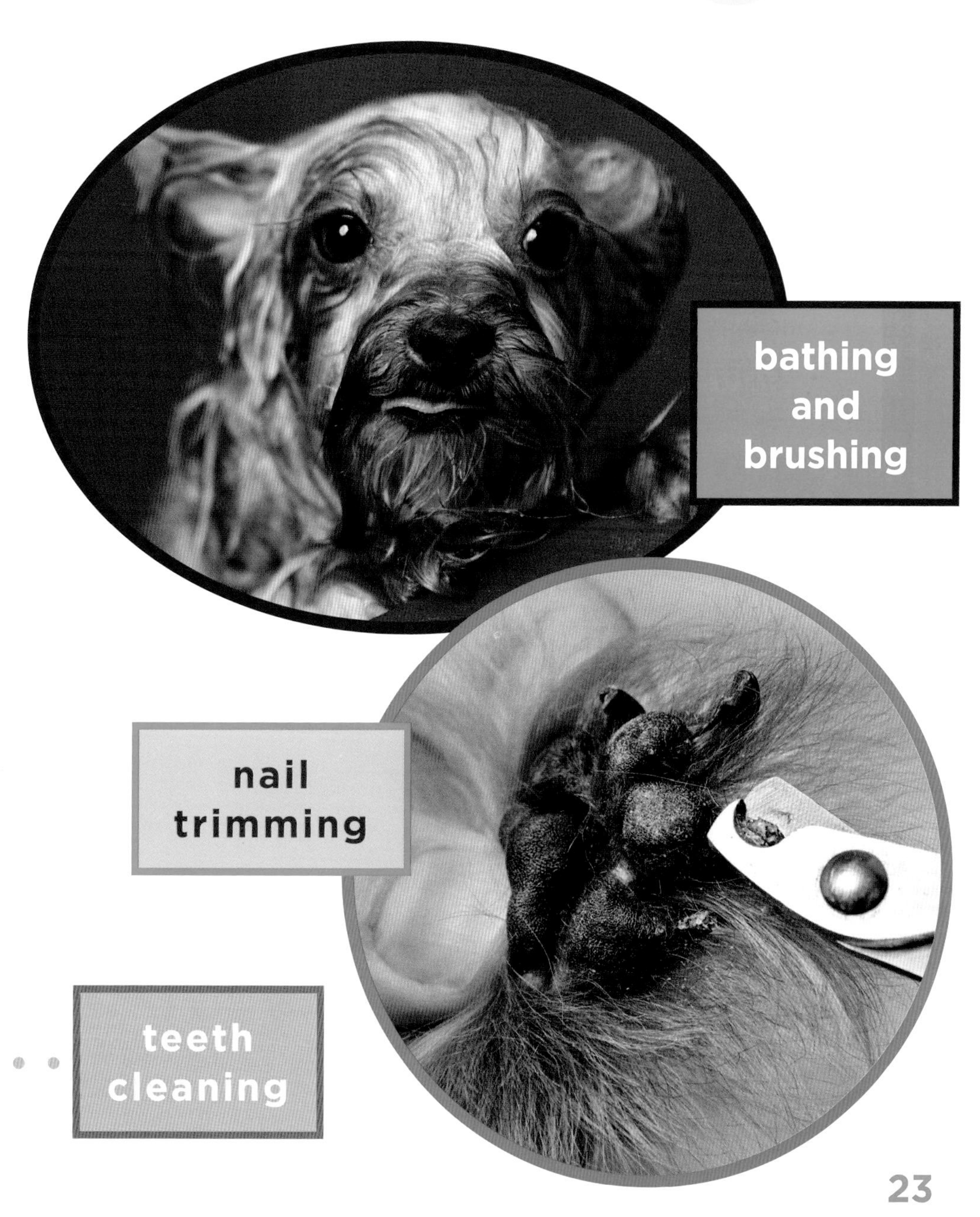

Eating and Exercising

Yorkies are **energetic** dogs. They enjoy short walks if the weather is nice. If it's too cold outside, they can run around a living room. They also enjoy playing fetch.

Yorkies, like other small dogs, don't need much to eat. They need about ¼ to ½ cup of dog food a day. The food should be split between two meals.

Yorkies don't shed much. They make good pets for people with allergies.

A Perky, Loyal Pet

Yorkshire terriers are excellent pets for many people. They are cute, cuddly, and full of fun. Yorkies need gentle, patient owners. But Yorkie owners say their pups are worth the effort.

QUIZ

Is a Yorkshire Terrier

Answer the questions below. Then add up your points to see if a Yorkie is a good fit.

1 Does it bother you when a dog barks?

A. Barking is the worst! **(1 point)**

B. As long as it's not all the time, I'm OK. **(2 points)**

C. Not at all! **(3 points)**

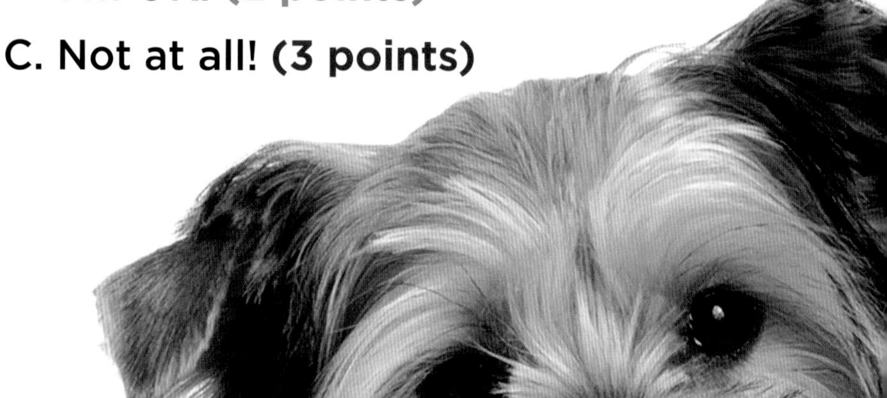

2 Do you want a tough dog?

A. Yes! I want to wrestle! **(1 point)**

B. It'd be nice to have a cuddle and jogging buddy. **(2 points)**

C. I'd rather brush my dog than roughhouse. **(3 points)**

3 How do you feel about grooming a dog?

A. I don't have time! **(1 point)**

B. It's OK, I guess. **(2 points)**

C. I can't wait to pick out hair bows together! **(3 points)**

3 points
A Yorkie is not your best match.

4–8 points
You like Yorkies, but another breed might be better for you.

9 points
A Yorkshire terrier would be a great buddy for your life!

GLOSSARY

adolescent (ad-oh-LES-uhnt)—a young person or animal that is developing into an adult

allergy (AL-er-jee)—a medical condition that causes someone to become sick after eating, touching, or breathing something that is harmless to most people

dislocate (DIS-loh-keyt)—to move a bone out of place

energetic (en-er-JET-ik)—having a lot of energy

habit (HAH-bet)—a usual way of behaving

loyal (LOY-uhl)—having complete support for someone or something

prance (PRANS)—to walk or move in a lively manner

silky (SIL-kee)—smooth and soft

BOOKS

Bozzo, Linda. *I Like Yorkshire Terriers!* Discover Dogs with the American Canine Association. New York: Enslow Publishing, 2017.

Gray, Susan H. *Yorkshire Terriers.* All about Dogs. New York: AV2 by Weigl, 2017.

Schuh, Mari. *Yorkshire Terriers.* Awesome Dogs. Minneapolis: Bellwether Media, 2016.

WEBSITES

Yorkshire Terrier
www.animalplanet.com/tv-shows/dogs-101/videos/yorkshire-terrier/

Yorkshier Terrier
www.dogster.com/dogbreed/yorkshire-terrier

Yorkshire Terrier (Yorkie)
www.akc.org/dog-breeds/yorkshire-terrier/

INDEX